Provinces and Territories of Canada

BRITISH COLUMBIA

— *"The Best Place on Earth"* —

Published by Weigl Educational Publishers Limited
6325 10 Street SE
Calgary, Alberta
T2H 2Z9

www.weigl.com

Library and Archives Canada Cataloguing in Publication data available upon request.
Fax 403-233-7769 for the attention of the Publishing Records department.

ISBN 978-1-55388-973-1 (hard cover)
ISBN 978-1-55388-986-1 (soft cover)

Printed in the United States of America
1 2 3 4 5 6 7 8 9 0 13 12 11 10 09

Editor: Heather C. Hudak
Design: Terry Paulhus

Weigl acknowledges Getty Images as its primary image supplier for this title.
British Columbia Archives: page 38 left; Detail of British Columbia Archives: page 38 right.

We gratefully acknowledge the financial support of the Government of Canada through the Book Publishing Industry Development Program
(BPIDP) for our publishing activities.

Contents

British Columbia 4

Land and Climate 8

Natural Resources 10

Plants and Animals.....................12

Tourism 16

Industry 18

Goods and Services......................20

First Nations 24

Explorers 26

Early Settlers 28

Population.................................32

Politics and Government...............34

Cultural Groups 36

Arts and Entertainment...............38

Sports 40

Canada 44

Brain Teasers 46

More Information........................47

Index 48

British Columbia

B ritish Columbia is Canada's westernmost province. It stretches from the Pacific Ocean in the West to the towering heights of the Rocky Mountains in the East. Some of the world's most beautiful scenery lies within the province's borders. Endless chains of snowcapped mountains, sea-battered shorelines, rolling grasslands, ancient rain forests, and sparkling waters all help to make British Columbia's landscape the most varied in the country. British Columbia is known around the world for its natural beauty. Visitors from near and far come to the province to explore some of the oldest trees, highest mountains, and most powerful rivers in North America. Adding to British Columbia's natural beauty are charming towns, bustling cities, busy ports, thriving businesses, and about 4.5 million residents.

Mount Assiniboine Provincial Park includes 39,050 hectares of land. It is part of the Canadian Rocky Mountain UNESCO World Heritage Site.

Vancouver is the largest city in British Columbia.

British Columbia covers about 947,800 square kilometres. It is the third-largest province in Canada, after Ontario and Quebec. Victoria is the capital of British Columbia. It is located on Vancouver Island.

The province shares its northern border with the Yukon and the Northwest Territories. Alberta is its neighbour to the east, and the U.S. states of Washington, Idaho, and Montana border the southern part of the province. The state of Alaska borders the northwestern part of British Columbia, and the Pacific Ocean makes up the rest of the western border. British Columbia is the only province that borders the Pacific Ocean.

The first European explorers arrived in British Columbia in the late 18th century. Since then, people have come from many different countries, and from other parts of Canada, to make their homes in the province.

In the Haida language, a protected region of the Queen Charlotte Islands is known as *Gwaii Haanas*, which means "Place of Wonder."

Almost one-third of Canada's fresh water is in British Columbia.

For thousands of years before the first explorers arrived, countless First Nations peoples inhabited the British Columbia region. These early Aboriginal Peoples lived on the abundant resources that the area had to offer.

Today, descendants of these early groups still live in the province. They, along with other ethnic groups in British Columbia, work hard to maintain the customs and traditions of their ancestors.

The longest railway tunnel in North America is located in British Columbia. In 1988, the Canadian Pacific Railway opened the Mount Macdonald Tunnel, which runs for 14.7 kilometres.

BC Ferries operates one of the largest ferry systems in the world. It has twenty-five routes between the Lower Mainland, Vancouver Island, and various coastal ports.

In Nelson, one of British Columbia's many mountain communities, residents live among the province's wildlife and rugged wilderness. Opportunities for outdoor adventure lie just beyond their front doors.

David Suzuki, a well-known scientist and environmentalist, lives in Vancouver.

LAND AND CLIMATE

This Thompson-Okanagan region accounts for most of Canada's fruit output, from apples, pears, and plums to cherries and apricots.

British Columbia's landscape is made up of dense rain forests, rolling plateaus, lush farmland, and hundreds of islands. There are six regions throughout the province. The Islands, which lie off the southwest corner of the province, make up one region. The largest and most populated island in this region is Vancouver Island. Victoria is on the southern part of Vancouver Island.

Another region is the Lower Mainland. The busy city of Vancouver is found there, along with the lush Fraser Valley, the Sunshine Coast, and the resort town of Whistler. Farther east lies the Thompson-Okanagan region, where a long growing season, mild winters, and abundant lakes create ideal conditions for growing fruit.

The Cariboo-Chilcotin region lies in the centre of the province's interior. It encompasses the Cariboo Mountains, as well as huge open areas of rangeland. In the southeast corner of the province lies the Kootenay region, known for its long lakes, hot springs, and friendly mountain communities.

Some of the mountain ranges in British Columbia include the Kootenays, the Selkirks, the Monashee, and the Cariboo.

British Columbia's final region is known as Northern British Columbia. It encompasses more than 50 percent of the province's land mass. The Queen Charlotte Islands are part of this region, as well as communities such as Prince Rupert, Dawson Creek, and Fort Nelson.

There are also a number of mountain ranges in the province. The Coast Mountains run along the west coast. They stretch from the Yukon border almost to the United States border in the south, and give the mainland a high, rugged coastline. The Coast Mountains protect the Lower Mainland and the coast from the arctic chill that comes from the north in the winter. On the east side of the Coast Mountains, the climate is very different. There, the ocean does not moderate the temperature. The interior is dry and hot in the summer and cold in the winter.

Many people enjoy climbing British Columbia's mountains.

Along British Columbia's easterly border, running almost **parallel** to the Coast Mountains, are the Rockies. In between the Rocky Mountains and the Coast Mountains lie several other mountain ranges.

NATURAL RESOURCES

Most of British Columbia is not suitable for growing crops due to the province's many mountains and forests. However, the Lower Fraser Valley and southern interior valleys have rich soils that are ideal for farming.

British Columbia's land **yields** a wealth of natural resources. Extensive forests, abundant minerals, and powerful water sources are all found within the province.

More than half of British Columbia is covered in forest. Logs, lumber, and other forest products have been a major contributor to the economy for a long time. Today, about 95 percent of the forest land is owned by the provincial government, and laws are in place to limit the number of trees that logging companies may cut down. People work hard to help preserve British Columbia's forests for wildlife, recreation, and as a resource for future generations.

British Columbia's dense forests are home to an abundance of wildlife.

KEEP CONNECTED

The first oil well in British Columbia was drilled near Fort St. John. To learn more about oil and gas in British Columbia, visit **www.ogc.gov.bc.ca**.

The province's rivers, lakes, and coastal waters are home to countless fish, including numerous species of salmon.

Most of British Columbia lies within the Western **Cordillera**, a geological formation that contains many important minerals, including gold, sulphur, copper, silver, zinc, and lead. Coal and natural gas are the province's most profitable minerals. Both are exported to other provinces and countries for the purpose of energy production.

A large portion of British Columbia's own energy comes from its water. The province's heavy rainfall and steep mountains result in fast-flowing rivers. These rivers provide great potential for **hydroelectric** power. The Brilliant Dam uses the power of the Kootenay River to produce electricity.

About 95 percent of British Columbia's electricity comes from hydroelectric plants.

PLANTS AND ANIMALS

Cypress and hemlock trees grow in British Columbia's Sechelt Peninsula.

Pacific dogwood was adopted in 1956 as British Columbia's provincial flower. Pacific dogwood is actually a tree. It can grow up to 8 metres high, and it flowers in April and May.

Trees can be found just about everywhere in British Columbia. The temperate rain forests on the west coast are home to some of the tallest and oldest trees in Canada. Western hemlock, Sitka spruce, and Douglas fir trees live in the coastal areas and on the offshore islands. Western red cedar, which became the provincial tree in 1988, also thrives here. This is because of the area's mild climate and large amount of rainfall. Some of these trees have grown more than 90 metres tall, while others have managed to live for over 800 years. Different trees grow in the interior regions of the province. Ponderosa pines, lodgepole pines, and western larches are all common in the drier areas of the interior, and Engelmann spruce trees cover the higher elevations of the mountains.

Trees are not the only plants that flourish in British Columbia. The province has an enormous variety of plants and shrubs, including cactus and sagebrush, in the dry areas, and fascinating grasses in the rolling prairies. In the summer, wildflowers of every colour decorate the alpine meadows. Daisies, lupines, wild roses, paintbrushes, and columbines are just a sampling of the flowers that light up many fields during the short alpine summers.

Every year, thousands of grey whales can be seen migrating on a route along the west coast of Vancouver Island.

British Columbia's diverse **topography** provides a wide variety of habitats for all kinds of wildlife. The province has more species of birds and mammals than any other area in Canada.

Grizzly bears, moose, elk, deer, wolves, and black bears all roam the many forests. Mountain goats and bighorn sheep are common in mountainous areas, and wild cats, such as cougars, lynxes, and bobcats, live in many of the province's wilderness regions.

A number of birds frequent British Columbia's air and waterways. Albatrosses, puffins, gulls, and cormorants are some of the many sea birds that thrive along the coast. Ducks, trumpeter swans, and blue grouse are all abundant throughout the province, and at least one-quarter of the world's bald eagles make their homes in British Columbia. The Steller's jay was voted the most popular bird by the people of British Columbia and became the provincial bird in 1987.

The number of bald eagles in British Columbia has increased over the past few years due to the ban on harmful pesticides.

The cougar is the largest wildcat native to British Columbia.

Among British Columbia's smaller mammals are beavers, porcupines, raccoons, marmots, rabbits, squirrels, and chipmunks.

Porpoises, dolphins, orcas, and humpback whales can often be seen frolicking in the coastal waters. They share these waters with sea otters and colonies of seals and sea lions. Five species of salmon dwell in the coast as adults, but move to freshwater streams and rivers to lay their eggs. British Columbia's fresh water is home to more than 70 other species of fish.

GET THE FACTS

Many animals west of the Coast Mountains have developed differently from their relatives east of the mountains. For example, coastal black bears are larger than those found in the interior.

There are 16 species of bats in British Columbia—more than any other province in Canada.

Cathedral Grove is home to a beautiful 800-year-old Douglas fir forest. Fishing facilities, hiking trails, and an Interpretative Centre make the forest a popular place to visit.

British Columbia is the birthplace of Greenpeace, one of the largest environmental groups in the world.

British Columbia has more than 675 parks and protected areas.

The southern interior valley of the Okanagan contains a desert, complete with cacti and rattlesnakes.

TOURISM

British Columbia's breathtaking wilderness draws visitors from all over the world. Countless lakes, towering mountains, lush forests, secluded islands, sandy beaches, and mild weather all serve to make the province a natural paradise for tourists. With beautiful scenery around every corner, and plenty of parkland, British Columbia is a perfect spot for all outdoor enthusiasts.

Within British Columbia's natural surroundings lie busy cities and charming towns that attract many visitors. Bordered by ocean and mountains, Vancouver is often regarded as one of the most beautiful cities in the world. It has many shops, restaurants, and attractions to offer its visitors.

Among the most popular attractions is Stanley Park, a large **peninsula** of old-growth forest and gardens. Stanley Park is home to the Vancouver Aquarium, where visitors can observe more than 8,000 aquatic animals and learn about British Columbia's marine life.

Pools filled with water from Rocky Mountain hot springs are popular with tourists and residents.

Victoria is another popular tourist destination. The provincial capital has a number of interesting sights to see. The Royal British Columbia Museum is one of Canada's most visited museums. It houses amazing displays of natural history, complete with the sounds and smells of nature. Tourists also know Victoria for its gardens. The most famous ones are the Butchart Gardens, where more than 5,000 varieties of flowers thrive.

British Columbia's natural hot springs draw many visitors. Among the most popular hot-spring resorts are Harrison Hot Springs, Radium Hot Springs, and Fairmont Hot Springs.

Located on the slopes of the Cariboo Mountain Range, Bowron Lake Provincial Park has many lakes and waterways that are ideal for canoeing.

KEEP CONNECTED

The Official Tourism Site of British Columbia has a variety of information about Vancouver, Victoria, and other destinations around the province. Check it out at www.hellobc.com.

INDUSTRY

British Columbia produces more lumber than any other Canadian province.

A large portion of British Columbia's economy relies on the use of natural resources. One of the most important resource-based industries in the province is forestry. Most of the trees harvested are used to make pulp and paper products or lumber.

Mineral resources also make a major contribution to the economy. About 30 kinds of valuable minerals are **extracted** from the land, including important metals and structural minerals used in the construction industry. Coal, petroleum, and natural gas also help to fuel the province's economy.

Fishing is another major resource-based industry in British Columbia. The province's commercial fish farms produce valuable crops of salmon, herring, halibut, cod, and sole. Canned and fresh fish are exported to markets all over the world. Fish is only one of the many foods that contribute to the province's food-processing industry. Beef, pork, fruit, and vegetable products are also manufactured in British Columbia.

Spot prawns are harvested in Prince Rupert.

Only about 3 percent of the province's land is fit for farming, but the farmland that does exist is so productive that agriculture is one of British Columbia's most important industries.

GOODS AND SERVICES

British Columbia's manufacturing activities are centred mostly in the Vancouver area and on the east coast of Vancouver Island.

The coastal community of Bella Coola is separated from the rest of the province by the Coast Mountains.

British Columbia has excellent shipping facilities. Goods are transported to and from the province by water, rail, road, and air. Water transportation is very efficient in British Columbia. The province has many year-round ports that host a wide range of freighters, fishing boats, and other vessels from many different countries. Vancouver's port is one of the largest and busiest ports in North America. It has terminals handling everything from coal and petroleum to forest, mineral, and agricultural products yielded from the province.

British Columbia's mountains make it hard to build railways and roads. For this reason, efficient land transportation took a long time to develop. Today, the province has more than 6,800 kilometres of rail and about 42,000 kilometres of roads. The Canadian Pacific Railway, CN Rail, and BC Rail all operate freight trains through the province, and truckers use many of the roadways to transfer goods.

Sparse settlement and challenging terrain have made road building very expensive in some regions, and there are still large areas of the province that have no roads. In fact, British Columbia has fewer highways than most of Canada's other regions. People who live in hard-to-reach communities often have goods brought to them by airplane or helicopter. Until the 1950s, there was no road leading into Bella Coola. The community's residents built the road after they grew tired of waiting for the government to build it.

The University of British Columbia is located on Vancouver's Point Grey, overlooking Georgia Strait. It is the largest univers in the province.

Education is an important service. British Columbia offers education from kindergarten to Grade 12, with many public and private schools for students and parents to choose from The province is also home to a wide variety of post-secondary programs.

Several community colleges and technic schools offer excellent training programs for students interested in specific fields.

Trains running through British Columbia carry goods and people into and out of the province. At one time, the Royal Hudson Steam Train was used for special excursions.

s well, there are 16 universities in British Columbia. They are the University of British Columbia, Simon Fraser University, Quest University, University of Phoenix, Fairleigh Dickinson University, Capilano University, and the Emily Carr University of Art & Design all located in the lower mainland. Kwantlen Polytechnic University, University of the Fraser Valley, and Trinity Western University are located in the Fraser Valley. On Vancouver Island you can find Royal Roads University, University of Victoria, Vancouver Island University, and University Canada West. There is only one university in the Okanagan and that is Thompson Rivers University and only one in Northern BC, University of Northern BC.

The largest **sector** of British Columbia's economy is the service industry. About 70 percent of the workers in British Columbia provide services for other people. Businesses in the service industry include health care, restaurants, legal services, computer services, hotels, and repair shops.

Thousands of people work in restaurants in British Columbia.

The Vancouver area is Western Canada's leading financial centre.

In addition to Canada's 5 percent goods and services tax, British Columbia has a 7 percent sales tax.

About 150 newspapers are published in British Columbia. The *Victoria Gazette* was the province's first newspaper. It was first published in 1858.

FIRST NATIONS

The first people to live in British Columbia inhabited the region more than 10,000 years ago. These early peoples lived in small groups and survived by fishing and hunting.

As the centuries wore on, these groups developed into larger, more distinct societies. By the 18th century, when the first European explorers arrived, there were an estimated 25,000 Aboriginal Peoples living throughout British Columbia.

Among the groups living on the coast were the Tsimshian, Kwakwaka'wakw, Haida, Tlingit, Nootka, and Coast Salish. Each of these coastal groups had its own traditions, but they also shared a common way of life. Coastal nations had permanent homes called **longhouses**. Carvings and paintings often decorated the walls and posts of these houses, and totem poles often stood out front. Totem poles represented family histories or Aboriginal legends. The oldest standing totem pole in the world is at the village of Kitwancool. It is known as "Hole-through-the-ice." Life was more difficult for the Aboriginal Peoples who lived in the interior. The weather was colder than at the coast, and finding food was more of a challenge.

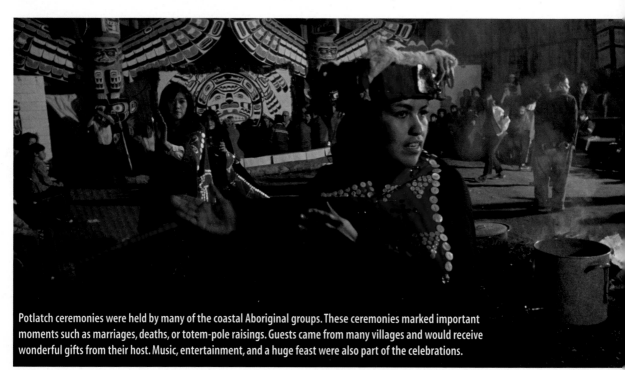

Potlatch ceremonies were held by many of the coastal Aboriginal groups. These ceremonies marked important moments such as marriages, deaths, or totem-pole raisings. Guests came from many villages and would receive wonderful gifts from their host. Music, entertainment, and a huge feast were also part of the celebrations.

The First Nations people of the interior were less settled than the coastal societies. They moved with the change of seasons and the availability of food. Among the people of the interior were the Interior Salish, the Athabaskans, and the Kootenay.

Nuu-chah-nulth refers to 18 First Nations that live in the Pacific Northwest.

More than 34 different languages are spoken among British Columbia's First Nations.

In Hazeltown, the Gitkskan re-create their early Aboriginal villages at the 'Ksan Historical Village.

EXPLORERS

Captain James Cook arrived on Vancouver Island's west coast in 1778.

British Columbia was the last of Canada's provinces to be visited by Europeans. In 1774, a Spanish explorer named Juan Perez Hernandez became the first European to see the region. A violent storm made it impossible for Hernandez to actually land on the shore. Despite this, he claimed the British Columbia coast as part of the Spanish Empire.

Four years later, a British explorer named Captain James Cook landed at Nootka Sound on Vancouver Island's west coast. He ignored Spain's earlier claim and declared the area part of the British Empire. Cook's crew began trading with Aboriginal Peoples in the area. They traded clothes and weapons for otter skins. Soon, a profitable fur-trading industry was established, attracting many other explorers and mapmakers.

While many explorers were mapping the coast, others were charting the region's interior. The first European to explore British Columbia's interior was Alexander Mackenzie, a fur trader with Montreal's North West Company.

Mackenzie was looking for a fur-trading route to the Pacific Ocean. In 1793, he entered the British Columbia region from the east by travelling up the Peace River. He and his crew travelled over the mountains and finally reached the Pacific Ocean at the Bella Coola Inlet.

Explorers often used a tool called a sextant to navigate the seas.

From 1792 to 1794, Captain George Vancouver explored and mapped the Pacific Coast. He and his crew named many parts of the area.

Simon Fraser followed the Fraser River to the sea in 1808, and David Thompson followed the Columbia River to its mouth in 1811. Both men opened fur-trading posts as they travelled.

The rivalry between the Hudson's Bay Company and the North West Company ended in 1821 when the two companies merged.

Other members of the North West Company explored the interior after Alexander Mackenzie.

GET THE FACTS

EARLY SETTLERS

In 1821, the two major fur-trading companies in British North America, the Hudson's Bay Company and the North West Company, merged to form one big company under the Hudson's Bay Company name.

The Canadian Pacific Railway's last stop was the small community of Vancouver. As a result, Vancouver grew into a major port city.

British Columbia's landscape, with its towering mountains and dense forests, slowed the coming of European settlers. For many decades, the only Europeans who spent time in the area were fur traders. During the first half of the 19th century, fur traders set up posts along the coast and on the main river routes.

In 1843, the Hudson's Bay Company founded Fort Victoria on the southern tip of Vancouver Island. By 1849, the British government made Vancouver Island a colony. In 1851, James Douglas, an official of the Hudson's Bay Company, was named governor of the colony. The colony of Vancouver Island remained largely unknown to the rest of the world for several years. Then, in the mid-1850s, gold was discovered in the Fraser River region of British Columbia's mainland.

Word of the discovery spread, and in 1858, thousands of gold-seekers came by boat from California and other areas. They stopped at Fort Victoria to buy supplies and request transportation to the mainland. Other **prospectors** travelled to the mainland on foot or by horse and wagon. In just a few months, about 30,000 hopeful miners had poured into the interior. Mining communities sprang up along the Lower Fraser River.

As thousands of miners made their way to the mainland, British authorities felt they had to strengthen their claim on the region. In 1858, they formed the mainland colony of British Columbia and appointed James Douglas as governor.

In 1866, Vancouver Island was united with the new colony to form one large colony under the name British Columbia. By this time, no more gold could be found in the region, and most of the miners had left. Other settlers stayed on and began farming on Vancouver Island and in the Lower Fraser Valley.

In 1867, the eastern part of Britain's North American colonies came together to form one large dominion—Canada. This act was called Confederation, and British Columbia was invited to join. The eastern provinces believed that making British Columbia a province of Canada would help to balance the power of the United States to the south.

Some of the early mining communities in the British Columbia region included Yale, Hope, New Westminster, and Barkerville. These settlements had restaurants, saloons, theatres, barber shops, and many other services.

In 1871, British Columbia became part of Canada, and the Canadian government agreed to build a railway linking the west to the east. Building the Canadian Pacific Railway was difficult, and it took until 1885 before it reached British Columbia. Construction of other railways and roads soon followed, opening up central parts of the province and helping to speed up development of the lumber, mining, and farming industries. Soon, settlers from other parts of Canada, and from England, began arriving in the province, attracted by the growing job prospects.

When the gold rush happened in British Columbia, Fort Victoria's population grew very quickly. During the first summer of the gold rush, 225 buildings were built in six weeks.

GET THE FACTS

The gold rushes led to the development of new transportation routes. The most impressive route was the Cariboo Road, which was built to link Yale to Barkerville. The road was completed in 1865 and made travel by wagon and stagecoach much easier. Settlers began using the road to reach communities in the interior.

James Douglas served as the governor of Vancouver Island for 13 years.

POPULATION

There are about 4.5 million people living in British Columbia. The southwestern corner of the province is the most heavily populated. This is because more than half of British Columbia's residents live in the Lower Mainland.

Vancouver, Burnaby, and Surrey are among the large communities that make up the Vancouver metropolitan area on the Lower Mainland. Large populations can also be found on the southeastern tip of Vancouver Island, where Victoria and its surrounding communities welcome new residents.

People from all over the world have moved to British Columbia. Many people come from other Canadian provinces, while others have immigrated from countries such as the United States or England.

About half of the people living in the province have some British ancestry, but substantial numbers of British Columbians are of Chinese, German, or French descent. The top 10 languages spoken by British Columbians are English, Chinese, Punjabi, German, French, Dutch, Italian, Tagalog, Spanish, and Korean.

Victoria is the retirement capital of Canada. Many people of retirement age are drawn to the city's mild climate and pleasant surroundings.

Aboriginal Peoples make up about 4.5 percent of British Columbia's population.

KEEP CONNECTED

Vancouver's downtown region is densely populated. Tall office towers and apartment buildings are needed to accommodate all of the city's people and businesses. To find out more about British Columbia's population, visit **www.bcstats.gov.bc.ca/ DATA/pop/popstart.asp.**

POLITICS AND GOVERNMENT

British Columbia was the fifth province to join Confederation. It became part of the Dominion of Canada in 1871.

L ike all of the provinces in Canada, British Columbia has three levels of government. These are federal, provincial, and local.

At the federal level, British Columbians elect 36 members of Parliament to the House of Commons in Ottawa. The federal government also appoints six senators to represent the province.

British Columbia is divided into 75 legislative **constituencies**. Residents of each constituency elect one representative to the Legislative Assembly.

Gordon Campbell was first elected premier of British Columbia in 2001. Campbell and other premiers meet at first ministers conferences to discuss issues of importance to the people they represent.

British Columbia's legislative buildings are located in Victoria. They have served as the seat of the provincial government since 1898.

The leader of the political party with the largest number of elected members becomes the premier of British Columbia. The premier then chooses a Cabinet, or executive council, from the elected members of the party.

The Legislative Assembly makes the laws that govern the province, and the premier and his Cabinet are responsible for carrying out these laws. At the local level of government, British Columbians elect mayors or councillors to **administer** to their cities, towns, villages, and district municipalities.

Canada's first female prime minister, Kim Campbell, is from Port Alberni, British Columbia. She served as prime minister from June 1993 to October 1993.

CULTURAL GROUPS

People in Vancouver celebrate Chinese New Year with parades, dragon dances, and other cultural events.

British Columbians have many different ethnic backgrounds and cultural traditions. Chinese people are a significant non-European ethnic group in the province. Many Chinese immigrants came to British Columbia in the 19th century to **pan** for gold, while others came as labourers during the construction of the Canadian Pacific Railway. Today, descendants of these early immigrants still make their homes in British Columbia. Vancouver's Chinatown is the second-largest Chinese community in North America, and Victoria's Chinatown is the oldest in Canada. Both communities celebrate Chinese heritage with pride.

Another cultural group that came to Canada in the 19th century are the Doukhobors, a Christian group from Russia. The Doukhobors are **pacifists**. In 1895, they refused to serve in the Russian army. The Russian government then denied their citizenship and put many in detention camps. A large group of Doukhobors immigrated to Canada where they were free to practise their beliefs. In the early 1900s, many moved from Saskatchewan to British Columbia. They settled throughout the Kootenays, especially in the Castlegar area. Today, descendants of the early Doukhobors still live in the Kootenays. Their culture is showcased in Castlegar's Doukhobor Village Museum.

The Dr. Sun Yat-Sen Classical Chinese Garden in Vancouver was built using traditional Chinese methods. It was the first authentic Chinese classical garden to be built outside China.

Vancouver's Museum of Anthropology displays towering totem poles, ceremonial masks, intricate jewellery, and contemporary artwork.

British Columbia's Hindu and Sikh communities celebrate Diwali, the festival of lights, with fireworks.

British Columbia has the greatest diversity of Aboriginal Peoples of any region in Canada. The province is home to 197 First Nations. Many of the groups are dedicated to preserving and sharing their heritage. In Alert Bay, the Kwakwaka'wakw share their culture at the U'Mista Cultural Centre. This centre houses a ceremonial potlatch collection and helps to explain the meaning of the potlatch. The centre also teaches children in the area the language, culture, songs, and dances of the Kwakwaka'wakw.

In Duncan, the Cowichan Native Village shares the traditions of the Cowichan. Visitors to the village can see carvers at work and watch women knit authentic Cowichan sweaters. The traditional culture of the Shuswap is shown at the Secwepemc Museum & Heritage Park in Kamloops. Haida culture is displayed at the Haida Gwaii Museum in Skidegate and at Vancouver's Museum of Anthropology, where visitors can walk around a reconstructed Haida Village. The Museum of Anthropology has the world's largest collection of arts and crafts of the Pacific Northwest Aboriginal Peoples.

ARTS AND ENTERTAINMENT

Many artists have found inspiration in British Columbia's scenery. Emily Carr, one of Canada's best-known artists, based her paintings on British Columbia's lush rain forests and on the Aboriginal culture in the province. Born in Victoria in 1871, Carr was associated with Canada's Group of Seven, who were known for their depictions of the Canadian landscape. Today, many of Emily Carr's paintings are featured at the Emily Carr Gallery in Victoria and at the Vancouver Art Gallery. Vancouver's gallery also features well-known contemporary painters from the province, including Jack Shadbolt, B.C. Binning, and Gordon Smith. British Columbia also inspires a variety of music.

The Emily Carr Institute of Art and Design is one of the top art schools in the country.

Theatre thrives in British Columbia. Vancouver is home to more than a dozen professional theatre companies. The Vancouver Playhouse Theatre Company presents both classical and modern plays, and the Arts Club Theatre Company is the largest regional company theatre in western Canada. In Victoria, the McPherson Playhouse and the Royal Theatre entertain audiences with comedies, musicals, and dramas. Smaller areas throughout the province have impressive community theatres. British Columbians who are interested in pursuing a career in the movies have an advantage over people living in other Canadian provinces.

British Columbia is one of the top centres for film and television production. Almost 200 films are shot in British Columbia every year. The province offers up some of the most varied scenery in the world. This, combined with Canada's lower production costs and a highly skilled work force, draws many filmmakers from Los Angeles and New York. British Columbia is full of talented actors, camera operators, makeup artists, special effects people, and other specialists that are needed when shooting a movie or television program. Many Canadian programs and movies have also been shot in the province.

Douglas Coupland is one of British Columbia's most famous writers. Others include Earle Birney and Dorothy Livesay.

The Santa Clause 2, which starred Elizabeth Mitchell and Tim Allen, was filmed in Vancouver.

SPORTS

Cycling through the province's many natural areas is a common pastime.

Many people in British Columbia enjoy sport fishing. Northern pike is a common catch. These fish grow to be more than 1.2 metres long.

British Columbia is a paradise for outdoor sports enthusiasts. With more than 450 provincial parks, six national parks, and countless regional, municipal, and city parks, the province has many exciting activities for everyone. Popular summer sports include hiking, mountain climbing, cycling, camping, golfing, fishing, and horseback riding. British Columbia's lakes, rivers, and coastal areas allow for virtually any water sport, including swimming, water-skiing, scuba diving, kayaking, river-rafting, and sailing.

The winter months offer up a whole new range of outdoor activities, including ice-fishing, snowmobiling, skating, snowshoeing, and skiing. British Columbia has some of the best ski hills in North America. Whistler, located in the southwest, is the most famous ski resort in the province. It is known around the world for its excellent downhill ski runs and cross-country trails, and for the many other winter activities that it has to offer. Other popular ski hills include Grouse Mountain, which lies only minutes from downtown Vancouver, Panorama Ski Resort in the Kootenay Mountains, and Red Mountain in Rossland.

Whistler is a popular tourist destination for many people. Aside from skiing, the area offers hiking trails and beautiful views.

Games such as soccer, lacrosse, hockey, baseball, and football are played at all levels throughout the province. A handful of professional sports teams are based in Vancouver. The Vancouver Canucks play in the National Hockey League, and the B.C. Lions play in the Canadian Football League.

Many excellent athletes have come out of British Columbia. Two of the province's most respected athletes are Terry Fox and Rick Hansen. Terry Fox was raised in Port Coquitlam. When he was 18 years old, he was diagnosed with bone cancer and had to have his right leg amputated above the knee. In 1980, Terry set out to run across Canada to raise money for cancer research.

Soccer is one of the summer sports enjoyed in British Columbia.

The West Coast Trail is a famous hiking trail. It is 77 kilometres long, and winds along Vancouver Island's untamed western shoreline. In order to reduce harmful environmental impact, only a limited number of hikers can use the trail at one time.

Every January, world-champion skiers come to Whistler to compete in the World Cup Freestyle Skiing Competition. In April, the Telus World Ski and Snowboard Festival brings thousands of snowboarders to Whistler.

After running more than 5,000 kilometres, Terry was forced to quit because his cancer had spread to his lungs. His dedication has inspired Canadians to donate millions of dollars to cancer research.

Rick Hansen was born in Port Alberni. In 1985, he set off in his wheelchair to travel 40,072 kilometres through 35 countries. His 792-day "Man in Motion Tour" raised $26 million for spinal cord research.

Every July, the city of Nanaimo holds the World Championship Bathtub Race. Motorized bathtubs race across the 58-kilometre stretch of the Georgia Strait, finishing at Departure Bay in Nanaimo.

The Vancouver Whitecaps FC are members of USL First Division in soccer, and the Vancouver Canadians are a Triple-A baseball team.

CANADA

Canada is a vast nation, and each province and territory has its own unique features. This map shows important information about each of Canada's 10 provinces and three territories, including when they joined Confederation, their size, population, and capital city. For more information about Canada, visit **http://canada.gc.ca**.

Alberta
Entered Confederation: 1905
Capital: Edmonton
Area: 661,848 sq km
Population: 3,632,483

British Columbia
Entered Confederation: 1871
Capital: Victoria
Area: 944,735 sq km
Population: 4,419,974

Manitoba
Entered Confederation: 1870
Capital: Winnipeg
Area: 647,797 sq km
Population: 1,213,815

New Brunswick
Entered Confederation: 1867
Capital: Fredericton
Area: 72,908 sq km
Population: 748,319

Newfoundland and Labrador
Entered Confederation: 1949
Capital: St. John's
Area: 405,212 sq km
Population: 508,990

SYMBOLS OF BRITISH COLUMBIA

FLAG　　　　**COAT OF ARMS**　　　　**FLOWER**
Pacific Dogwood

Map Labels

Baffin Bay

0 200 400 Kilometers
0 200 400 Miles

Baffin Island

Davis Strait

Iqaluit (Frobisher Bay)

Ivujivik

Labrador Sea

NEWFOUNDLAND

Schefferville

Happy Valley-Goose Bay

Island of Newfoundland

Chisasibi (Fort George)

Gander
Saint John's

QUEBEC

Sept-Iles

Gulf of St. Lawrence

St. Pierre and Miquelon (FRANCE)

posonee

Chibougamau

PRINCE EDWARD ISLAND

Sydney

NEW BRUNSWICK

Charlottetown

Quebec

Fredericton

Sherbrooke

Saint John

Halifax

Sudbury

Montreal

NOVA SCOTIA

Ottawa

Lake Huron

Lake Ontario

Toronto
Hamilton
London

Lake Erie

ANIMAL
Spirit Bear

TREE
Western Red Cedar

GEM
Jade

Province/Territory Info

Northwest Territories
Entered Confederation: 1870
Capital: Yellowknife
Area: 1,346,106 sq km
Population: 42,940

Nova Scotia
Entered Confederation: 1867
Capital: Halifax
Area: 55,284 sq km
Population: 939,531

Nunavut
Entered Confederation: 1999
Capital: Iqaluit
Area: 2,093,190 sq km
Population: 531,556

Ontario
Entered Confederation: 1867
Capital: Toronto
Area: 1,076,395 sq km
Population: 12,986,857

Prince Edward Island
Entered Confederation: 1873
Capital: Charlottetown
Area: 5,660 sq km
Population: 140,402

Quebec
Entered Confederation: 1867
Capital: Quebec City
Area: 1,542,056 sq km
Population: 7,782,561

Saskatchewan
Entered Confederation: 1905
Capital: Regina
Area: 651,036 sq km
Population: 1,023,810

Yukon
Entered Confederation: 1898
Capital: Whitehorse
Area: 482,443 sq km
Population: 33,442

BRAIN TEASERS

Test your knowledge of British Columbia by trying to answer these boggling brain teasers!

1 Multiple Choice

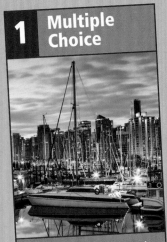

Which city is the largest in British Columbia?
a) Victoria
b) Vancouver
c) Kelowna
d) Prince George

2 Multiple Choice

The top ten languages spoken by British Columbians are English, Chinese, Punjabi, German, French, Dutch, Italian, Tagalog, Spanish, and

_____.
a) Japanese
b) Swedish
c) Korean
d) Russian

3 True or False?

The Pacific dogwood became the provincial flower in 1968.

4 True or False?

James Cook was the first European to see British Columbia.

5 True or False?

British Columbia became a province in 1920.

6 True or False?

Almost one-third of Canada's fresh water is in British Columbia.

7 Multiple Choice

How many provincial parks are in British Columbia?
a) exactly 127
b) about 685
c) more than 450

8 True or False?

Victoria is the capital of British Columbia.

MORE INFORMATION

GLOSSARY

administer: to direct or manage

constituencies: districts of people represented by an elected officer

cordillera: a chain of mountains

extracted: drawn out of the land

hydroelectric: electricity produced by the gathering of water power

longhouses: shared houses made of wood

pacifists: people who refuse to participate in military activity because of their beliefs

pan: to look for gold by washing gravel out in a pan

parallel: going in the same direction but never meeting

peninsula: an area of land that is almost completely surrounded by water

prospectors: people who search for gold

sector: a distinct part

temperate: neither too hot nor too cold

topography: the surface features of a place or region

yields: produces

BOOKS

Foran, Jill. *Canada's Land and People: British Columbia*. Calgary: Weigl Educational Publishers Limited, 2008.

Foran, Jill. *Canadian Sites and Symbols: British Columbia*. Calgary: Weigl Educational Publishers Limited, 2004.

Kissock, Heather. *Canadian Industries: Forestry*. Calgary: Weigl Educational Publishers Limited, 2007.

Ostopowich, Melanie. *Canadian Geographical Regions: The Cordillera*. Calgary: Weigl Educational Publishers Limited, 2006.

WEBSITES

Government of British Columbia
www.gov.bc.ca

British Columbia Travel and Tourism
www.travel.bc.ca

The Royal British Columbia Museum
www.royalbcmuseum.bc.ca/MainSite/default.aspx

Some websites stay current longer than others. To find information on Alberta, use your Internet search engine to look up such topics as "Alberta," "rodeo," "Rockies," "Prairie Provinces," or any other topic you want to research.

INDEX

Barkerville 17, 30, 31
Butchart Gardens 17

Canadian Pacific Railway
  7, 21, 29, 31, 36
Cariboo-Chilcotin 8
Carr, Emily 23, 38
Coast Mountains 9, 15, 21
Cook, James 26, 46

Douglas, James 29, 30, 31

education 22

fishing 15, 19, 24, 41
forestry 19
Fox, Terry 42, 43
Fraser River 27, 29

gold rush 17, 31
Greenpeace 15

Haida 6, 24, 37
Hansen, Rick 42, 43
hot springs 8, 17
Hudson's Bay Company
  27, 28, 29

Kamloops 37

Mackenzie, Alexander 27
Museum of Anthropology 37

Nanaimo 43, 46
North West Company 27, 28

Okanagan 8, 15

Pacific Ocean 4, 6, 27
Port Alberni 35, 43
potlatch 24, 37
Prince George 23, 46
Prince Rupert 9, 19

Queen Charlotte Islands
  6, 9, 37

rain forests 4, 8, 13, 38
Rocky Mountains 4, 9

Stanley Park 16

Vancouver 6, 7, 8, 16, 17, 20,
  21, 22, 23, 29, 32, 33, 36, 37,
  38, 39, 41, 42, 43, 46
Vancouver, Captain
  George 27
Vancouver Island 6, 7, 8, 14,
  20, 23, 26, 29, 30, 31, 32, 43
Victoria 6, 8, 17, 23, 29, 32,
  35, 36, 38, 39, 44, 46

Whistler 8, 41, 42, 43